The Hidden Treasures of Egypt

Rob Waring, *Series Editor*

HEINLE
CENGAGE Learning

Australia • Brazil • Japan • Korea • Mexico • Singapore • Spain • United Kingdom • United States

Words to Know

This story is set in Egypt. It takes place in the capital city of Cairo [kaɪroʊ].

Cairo *

EGYPT

EGYPT AFRICA

N
W——E
S

 A **The Egyptian Museum in Cairo.** Read the paragraph. Then complete the sentences with the correct forms of the underlined words.

The Egyptian Museum in Cairo holds a large number of artifacts from ancient Egypt. Among these precious objects are some of the mummies of ancient Egyptian pharaohs. These preserved bodily remains were most often taken from the leaders' tombs located within pyramids found throughout Egypt. Although the Egyptian Museum contains 160,000 artifacts, many of them the royal treasures of kings, only half of them are on display.

1. A _____ is a place where someone is put after they have died.

2. A _____ is a triangular building.

3. _____ are the ancient kings of Egypt.

4. A _____ person is related to a king or queen.

5. _____ are ancient pieces of art or objects of historical value.

6. A _____ is a dead body that has been preserved and wrapped in material.

The Ancient Pharaoh Tutankhamen

Leader of Egypt circa* 1333–1324 b.c.

- Tutankhamen is sometimes known as 'King Tut' or the 'boy king,' because he was a very young leader.
- He is known mainly due to the discovery of his undisturbed tomb in 1922.
- The tomb's artifacts are sometimes taken on tour, but are permanently held at the Egyptian Museum in Cairo.

*circa = approximately

B The Keepers of History. Read the paragraph. Then match each word with the correct definition.

Dr. Zahi Hawass [zɑhi həwɑs], one of Egypt's most well-known archaeologists, has been responsible for digging up a number of important ancient artifacts. His specialty is the study of Egypt, so this Egyptologist is now organizing a huge exhibit at the Egyptian Museum. The curator of the museum, El Ham Salah el-Din [ɛl hɑm sɑlɑ ɛl din], will choose many of the exhibits. Nadia Lokma [nɑdyɑ lɔkmɑ], a museum conservator, is going to prepare the exhibits for display and restore any damaged pieces.

1. archaeologist _____

2. Egyptologist _____

3. curator _____

4. conservator _____

a. a person whose job is to clean and repair historical works of art

b. the person in charge of a museum

c. a person who studies ancient Egyptian artifacts

d. a general term for a person who studies human life and civilizations, often by searching historical sites

Today, a large number of Egypt's greatest of historic discoveries do not lie far out in the deserts of Egypt. They lie in a much more surprising place: downtown Cairo. Tens of thousands of objects of rare beauty, mystery, and symbolic power have been gathered together in the Egyptian Museum of Cairo. The collection is composed of royal mummies, precious jewelry, and King Tutankhamen's treasures, as well as other artifacts representing the ideology and lifestyle from up to 5,500 years ago.

Now, this extraordinary museum is preparing for an exciting new exhibition. All in all, the museum probably contains the most extensive collection of ancient artifacts on Earth. But what most people don't know is that in the storage rooms of its huge basement, the museum holds many more treasures. These are the amazing hidden treasures of the Egyptian Museum that will soon be revealed in the new exhibition.

CD 1, Track 07

The Egyptian Museum in Cairo houses tens of thousands of ancient artifacts.

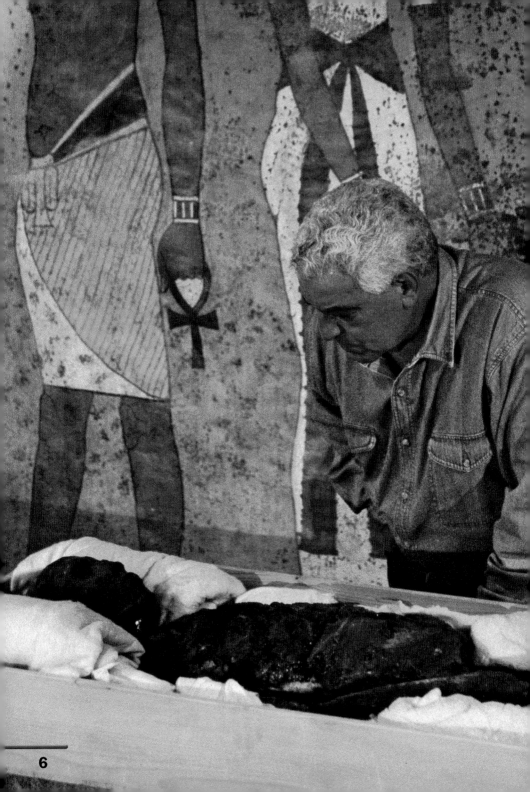

Dr. Zahi Hawass, Egypt's most well-known archaeologist, explains the idea behind the exhibition. Hawass is the Secretary General of the Supreme Council of Antiquities and the man who is ultimately responsible for the museum. He takes a moment to describe just how rich in artifacts the museum actually is. "[The] Cairo Museum may be the best museum in the world," he says, "because of the amazing artifacts that you can see and wonder [about] when you come to this museum. The history of mummies and King Tut and all of that; it's something that you can never see in any [other] museum in the world. And can you imagine that [the] Cairo Museum contains one hundred and sixty thousand artifacts, but only half of [them] are on display?" If only half of the artifacts are being viewed, that means that up to 80,000 objects are hidden away beneath the cool **marble**[1] floors of the institution.

---

[1]**marble:** a type of expensive stone that is cut and shined for use in floors, walls, statues, and decoration

The basement of the Egyptian Museum is truly a wonderful place for anyone interested in ancient Egypt or archaeology. It's a vast network of underground passages that is absolutely filled with priceless objects from the past. As he walks through the darkened rooms and past the corners filled with boxes of artifacts, Dr. Hawass explains just how much history is stored beneath the museum. "I don't think that any museum in the world would really have a basement like this," he says. "A place full of thousands [and] thousands [of] objects that came from excavations all over Egypt. And when you come by here and you walk around the galleries, you can smell history."

Infer Meaning

1. What does the word 'priceless' on page 8 mean? Look at the words around it and write a definition.

2. What does the word 'excavation' on page 8 mean? Look at the words around it and write a definition.

To give an example of the treasures found in the basement of the museum, Dr. Hawass opens a small wooden box that may contain evidence of what he calls the first **plastic surgery**[2] in history: an artificial toe. As he gently opens the container, Dr. Hawass describes the find. "Let me show you one of these amazing artifacts," he says and picks up a small dark object. "Look at [this foot]," he notes as he points to a mummified foot that is missing the largest toe, "It's the [foot] of a person that lived … three thousand years ago, and he lost his toe." Hawass continues as he holds a small wooden toe in front of the foot, "What the Egyptian[s] did, [is] they replaced it; they [performed] the first plastic surgery [that] ever happened in history!" Hawass then displays strings that tied the toe to the person. "They had this kind of thing to tie every piece of [the toe to the foot]," he says gesturing to the strings and artificial toe, "because they have holes here, and these holes would be tied [to the foot with string]."

The Egyptologist then explains that, like most Egyptians of the time, the man with the artificial toe probably believed in life after death, or 'the afterlife.' Because of this, the artificial toe was **buried**[4] with him, so that he would be able to walk in the next life. "The analysis showed that this man lived for a few years walking with this," he says. "And he kept it with him because he would like to walk safely in the afterlife." Items like this artificial toe reveal some fascinating information about what life—and death—was like in ancient Egypt.

---

[2] **plastic surgery:** an operation on the body to alter or improve its shape or appearance
[3] **bury:** put something (especially a dead person) in the ground

Of course, preparing for the new exhibition is a huge task, and involves the work of several of the museum's employees. El Ham Salah el-Din has been a museum curator for 15 years and now she's busy helping and organizing for the new exhibition. The theme of the show is 'Hidden Treasures' and many of these treasures are recorded in the pages of the museum's lengthy record books. The books are so old that the pages are falling apart, but El Ham is carefully searching through them for long forgotten artifacts, hidden in dark corridors of the basement. But what should she choose? She can't display them all and must exclude at least some of the items. In order to decide, she reads through the records and chooses some of the items before asking for them to be brought out so that she can inspect them.

As the pieces arrive, it's not hard to see that there is an incredible amount of history in the museum. It will be extremely challenging to decide what to put on display and which stories to tell. El Ham opens one of the boxes, carefully unhooking the lock and gently opening the top of the container. As she does so, she reveals an ocean of cotton protective wrapping, and selects one of the objects hidden within the box. The clear plastic box she carefully chooses holds an interesting find from a recent excavation: a 3,000-year-old **ivory palette**.[4] The palette, a small, flat, detailed piece in the shape of a fish, was used for mixing powders and beauty aids. As she examines the artifact, it is obvious how beautiful the piece is and how it provides an interesting view into everyday life all of those years ago. But there is more to be discovered inside the box. There is also an **ibex antelope**,[5] delicately made of **flint**,[6] which dates back more than 5,500 years. The scope of the exhibition is just too limited to include all of the amazing pieces that have lain in storage for decades. How can one decide which to display? How can one make one priceless piece a priority over another? The job is not an easy one and El Ham must inspect each artifact closely.

---

[4] **ivory palette:** a flat plate made of an elephant or other animal's horn used to mix thick liquids
[5] **ibex antelope:** a fast, four-legged animal with horns
[6] **flint:** a hard, gray stone used to make fire

One of the objects that has been chosen to appear in the 'Hidden Treasures' exhibition is a statue of an important **priest**[7] called 'Kai.' The statue is very beautiful and in extremely good condition. For most at the museum it is simply another fantastic addition to the show, but for others, this particular piece denotes a more special meaning. In 1999, Dr. Hawass was working at the Giza Plateau and discovered the statue of Kai. Dr. Hawass must now go back to the Giza Plateau to pick Kai up from the storage house for the exhibition. As he and an assistant drive up to the location, they are taken directly to the storage unit. While the caretaker unlocks the door, the two men wait nearby. At last the box that holds Kai is located and the workers break open the wooden top. Hawass personally unwraps the statue from the cotton that is used to protect it. After digging down into the protective material, Hawass can see that the ancient statue is safe.

The artifact is relatively small, but beautifully proportioned and very well preserved. The contrast of the colors and the quality of the work make the piece wonderful to view. The statue is of a young, handsome man seated on a chair, his right hand raised to his chest as if showing respect to an unknown person. The most striking elements of the statue are the eyes, which are wide open and lifelike. They're also what the great archaeologist remembers most when he thinks of the moment he first found the figure. "I remember when I found this statue," he says. "[When] my eyes came to look at the eyes of this statue. It was the most beautiful moment in my life."

---

[7] **priest:** someone who performs religious ceremonies and duties

In a search for new and unseen pieces to exhibit, Dr. Hawass has ordered regional storage facilities all over Egypt to be opened. Now, priceless artifacts from all over the country are flooding in to the Egyptian Museum to join the treasures found in the basement. From Aswan, Luxor, and the Nile Delta—some of Egypt's greatest archaeological sites—come large numbers of ancient pictures, statues, **inscriptions**[8] in stone, and **carvings**.[9]

None of the artifacts has ever been shown before, and there are moments of intense excitement as the researchers open the boxes and carefully unwrap them. For everyone involved, Hawass and El Ham included, this is an unforgettable opportunity. There's a lot of chatting and excitement as one box after another is opened, and strange and interesting artifacts are seen for the first time. People try to explain what things are, describe the stories on the carvings, and express their feelings about being some of the first people to see these treasures. Dr. Hawass probably sums up everyone's opinion best. "This exhibit will be incredible!" he says enthusiastically as he heads off to look at another piece.

---

[8]**inscription:** words that are written on or cut into stone or other substances
[9]**carving:** a piece of art that has been shaped by cutting it with exactness

Scan for Information

Scan pages 20 and 23 to answer the questions.

1. Why are some parts of the child mummy's body being removed?

2. Why is the photographer taking photographs of all the exhibits?

Before the exhibition starts, though, there is plenty of work to be done. After the artifacts arrive, they must subsequently be prepared for display in the museum where they will be exposed to the light, often for the first time in ages. Most of the objects have been lying in storage for many years—sometimes decades—and they need careful conservation, cleaning, and restoration. For example, in one of the preparation rooms, the statue of Kai is being wiped with a special liquid so that it will look its best for the exhibit. However, the artifact must be cleaned very carefully and in a special manner so that its delicate colors won't be harmed.

In another room, a child mummy, which was found inside a tomb at the Bahariya Oasis, is also being restored. The mummy had lain unseen for 2,000 years, so a museum conservator must now work carefully to prepare it for display. He must remove the parts of the body that have **decayed**[10] to keep the rest of the mummy protected. He works carefully, using a sharp knife to cut down the edges of the ancient body wrapped in material. It takes a lot of time, but it will be worth it once the piece is displayed beautifully at the new exhibition.

---

[10]**decay:** go bad; rot

Time is not only an element for the conservator fixing the damaged pieces. Time is also passing quickly for everyone and the exhibition opening date is approaching. As preparations for the exhibition continue, National Geographic photographer Ken Garrett arrives at the museum. His job will be to photograph the artifacts, thereby documenting each one. He talks about the thrill of it all, and about just how unexpected the daily work can be. "You have no idea what you're going to see when you come in here," he says. "Each day, more and more boxes come in, and we keep pulling back the cotton and rushing through this stuff."

As the curators rapidly view object after object and question whether or not they should be included in the show, the answer is often, "No. No. No." But then, once in a while, the curators find something that makes them say, "Ah! What's that?" or "[Do] you know?" as they try to find out if the piece can be included in the exhibit. According to Garrett, "It's like there's this constant train of pieces coming in."

There are several amazing aspects of the exhibit, but one of the most incredible things is just how well preserved many of the artifacts are. Garrett is currently photographing some extremely detailed jewelry, the colors of which are all still beautifully preserved— even after thousands of years. As he focuses in on the magnificent pieces in order to get just the right shot, he comments, "Thirty-five hundred years ago, and they're still in perfect condition."

Some of Tutankhamen's personal jewelry will also be included in the show, along with other objects found in the boy king's tomb. Many of the Pharaoh Tutankhamen's treasures have already been shown, but one of them has been lying in a box unseen since it arrived here in 1923. It is nothing less than the king's own **harness**[11] for his **chariot**,[12] made of leather and gold. On the harness, there are pictures showing scenes from the young king's life.

Museum conservator Dr. Nadia Lokma is preparing the pieces of the harness for the exhibition. As she reviews the pieces for the show, she takes a moment to describe one. She carefully lifts up the gold-covered leather object and points to a figure represented on it. "If you look here," she says, "you will find that the king, Tutankhamen, is on his chariot." As Dr. Lokma talks about the harness, it becomes obvious that such artifacts really make history come alive for her. "It's wonderful!" she claims. "It is like a story. It is like a story of the life of the king, his life as a human being, so I think it is wonderful. I love it!" Hopefully, when the public is able to see such artifacts in the exhibition, they too will gain some understanding of the boy king's life.

---

[11]**harness:** straps and neckwear that horses and other animals wear to pull loads
[12]**chariot:** a two-wheeled vehicle drawn by horses often used in ancient times

Fact or Opinion?

Read the following statements. Write 'F' for those that are factual or 'O' for those that are an opinion.

1. Some of Tutankhamen's magnificent jewelry will be included in the show. _____

2. On the harness are pictures showing scenes from the young king's life. _____

3. The harness is wonderful. _____

4. The harness will help people understand the boy king's life. _____

The new exhibition is almost ready, but one display case is still empty. Four thousand years after he was laid to rest beside the pyramids, it is time for Kai—Dr. Hawass's favorite piece—to reach his final destination. It's a special moment for Dr. Hawass, and he watches intensely as workers cautiously carry Kai to the museum and place him in the display case that has been prepared for his arrival. Like many archaeologists, Dr. Hawass's interest in the past is matched with an excitement for the future. He believes that there are many more artifacts still to be found in Egypt. "What is amazing," he says, "[is] that all these artifacts in the museum and the basement are **[the] tip of [the] iceberg**."[13]

Hawass realizes that there are thousands of interesting artifacts that are yet to be displayed, and countless more that are yet to even be discovered. Today, archaeologists around the world are continuing to devote their lives to finding artifacts from the past. Many wonderful objects have already been discovered, but no one knows what other hidden treasures may still lie beneath the sands of Egypt.

---

[13]**the tip of the iceberg:** *(expression)* a small evident part or aspect of something that is much larger, but which is mainly hidden

After You Read

1. Why are the treasures in this collection considered hidden?
   A. because they were buried in pyramids for a long time
   B. because archaeologists didn't want them to be visible
   C. because they haven't been exhibited for the public
   D. because they are the latest discoveries of Egyptologists

2. Which statement best expresses what Dr. Hawass says on page 7?
   A. The Egyptian Museum has more exhibits than any other museum in the world.
   B. The Egyptian Museum has an astonishing amount of historical artifacts.
   C. Many visitors wonder how many artifacts are in the museum's storeroom.
   D. Only the Egyptian Museum has mummies.

3. The word 'smell' on page 8 can be replaced by:
   A. sense
   B. precede
   C. attribute
   D. enhance

4. What is the main purpose of the example of the artificial toe?
   A. to introduce the topic of plastic surgery
   B. to prove how advanced the Egyptians were
   C. to talk about the religion of ancient Egypt
   D. to illustrate how artifacts teach about history

5. Which of the following is NOT an artifact mentioned in the story?
   A. the bones of a fish
   B. a dish for beauty products
   C. an animal sculpture
   D. a statue of a priest

6. In paragraph 1 on page 17, 'others' refers to:
   A. Egyptologists
   B. Dr. Hawass and his assistant
   C. visitors
   D. El Ham

7. According to the writer, Dr. Hawass is searching other storerooms because:
  A. He doesn't like the current selection for the exhibition.
  B. He is worried that another museum will try to hold a similar exhibition.
  C. He wants to guarantee that the exhibition has the most interesting pieces.
  D. He is trying to find a statue that is a companion for Kai.

8. Which of the following is a suitable heading for page 20?
  A. Restoration Overwhelming Museum Staff
  B. Cleaning Liquid Gives Color to Kai
  C. Child Mummy Accidentally Destroyed
  D. A Careful Process of Preservation

9. When the curator says, "No. No. No," they are demonstrating that:
  A. They don't want to see another box.
  B. They are rejecting most items.
  C. The cotton on the boxes was very dirty.
  D. Many items were broken when they unwrapped them.

10. Which of the following is NOT true about Tutankhamen?
  A. His picture is on a harness.
  B. He had a lot of jewelry.
  C. He was a very young leader.
  D. He died in 1923.

11. The word 'obvious' in paragraph 2 on page 24 means:
  A. implicit
  B. contrary
  C. rational
  D. apparent

12. What is the writer implying in the last sentence on page 26?
  A. Archaeologists don't have a lot of work to do in Egypt.
  B. There are many more hidden treasures all across Egypt.
  C. It's unlikely that anyone will make any more discoveries.
  D. Egypt's history will remain a secret buried deep in the desert.

Museum News
Traveling Exhibitions

● ●

In the past, if a person wanted to see the national treasures of a country, one had to go there in person. Therefore, very few people were able to enjoy some of history's most important and fascinating artifacts. This has changed with a recent increase in the number of traveling museum exhibitions. Today, more and more Ministries of Culture and federal government offices are allowing important historical and artistic works to be taken on around-the-world journeys to allow people everywhere to witness them with their own eyes.

KING TUTANKHAMEN ARTIFACTS

A traveling exhibition of artifacts from the tomb of King Tutankhamen, popularly known as 'King Tut,' toured the United States from November 1976 to April 1979. The 55 objects in this display were shown in six cities and were seen by around eight million museum-goers. A subsequent touring exhibit was launched in 2007, this time with 130 artifacts and stops in London and three different American cities. However some items, like the king's golden face mask, are too valuable or too delicate to be transported long distances, so 'replicas', or pieces that simulate the real piece, are featured in the show.

Sample of Items Traveling in the Tutankhamen Exhibition	
Symbols of Royalty	• King Tut's solid golden head piece • a solid gold knife and solid gold knife holder • a broad necklace of gold and jewels • King Tut's royal boyhood chair
Furniture	• wooden boxes, chests, and chairs
Everyday Items	• dog collars • perfume holders

Japanese Woodblock Prints

JAPANESE COLOR WOODBLOCK PRINTS

The University of Virginia Art Museum, in Charlottesville, Virginia, has an extraordinary collection of Japanese color woodblock prints. These prints document the period from about 1850 to 1900, a time when Japan was opening itself to Western influences. Before this point, Japan was a closed society that had little contact with the world outside of its borders. These works of art beautifully show the feeling of change and the trend toward modernization. The museum has put together a traveling exhibition of 60 of these prints, which can be borrowed and exhibited worldwide for periods of eight weeks or more.

FACE-TO-FACE WITH 'LUCY'

One of the world's most famous archaeological finds in history are the 3.2 million-year-old bones of a 106-centimeter-tall* female found in the Ethiopian desert in 1974. Lucy, a name given to her by the discovery team, is a 'hominid,' or a creature that scientists believe is a primitive ancestor of modern human beings. Anthropologists believe that human life began in this region, and Lucy is important to our understanding the evolution of humans. Rarely is an artifact this valuable allowed to travel widely, but Lucy has been taken to several museums in the U.S. while a detailed replica remains at the Ethiopian Natural History Museum.

*See page 32 for a metric conversion chart.

CD 1, Track 08

Word Count: 394
Time: _____

Vocabulary List

archaeologist (3, 7, 8, 17, 18, 26)
artifact (2, 3, 4, 7, 8, 11, 12, 15, 17, 18, 20, 23, 24, 26)
bury (11)
carving (18)
chariot (24)
conservator (3, 20, 23, 24)
curator (3, 12, 23)
decay (20)
Egyptologist (3, 11)
flint (15)
harness (24, 25)
ibex antelope (15)
inscription (18)
ivory palette (15)
marble (7)
mummy (2, 4, 7, 20)
pharaoh (2, 24)
plastic surgery (11)
priest (17)
pyramid (2, 26)
royal (2, 4)
the tip of the iceberg (26)
tomb (2, 20, 24)

Metric Conversion Chart

Area
1 hectare = 2.471 acres

Length
1 centimeter = .394 inches
1 meter = 1.094 yards
1 kilometer = .621 miles

Temperature
0° Celsius = 32° Fahrenheit

Volume
1 liter = 1.057 quarts

Weight
1 gram = .035 ounces
1 kilogram = 2.2 pounds